The Honey Pot Home

A gentle story about foster care, family, and feeling safe

Written by
Adorae Younge

Copyright © 2025, Adorae Younge

The Honey Pot Home

All rights reserved. No part of this book may be reproduced, stored in a retrieval system, or transmitted in any form or by any means, electronic, mechanical, photocopying, recording, or otherwise, without the prior written permission of the copyright owner.

Email: turningmirror@outlook.com

Book cover design, illustrations and layout by Christian Book Editor Ltd (christianbookeditor.uk)

FOREWORD

Dear Grown-Ups,

Thank you for buying **The Honey Pot Home**. This story was written for every child navigating the uncertainty of foster care, and for every adult walking beside them with love, patience, and hope.

Ruby's and Bobby's journey mirrors the quiet bravery of so many children whose lives are touched by change. In a world that can sometimes feel overwhelming, they remind us that safety, gentleness, and consistency matter more than we know.

This book is a gentle way to help young children understand what foster care is, and more importantly, that it's never their fault when grown-ups struggle. Whether you are a foster carer, social worker, adoptive parent, birth family member, teacher, or someone supporting a child through change — thank you. Your presence makes a difference.

Mr and Mrs Honey Pot symbolise the steady, nurturing spaces that children need while the big decisions are being made. The social workers, guardians, and judges represent the network of adults working to keep children safe and heard. And at the heart of it all is the hope that every child will know they are precious, wanted, and never alone.

May this story be a bridge to healing conversations, quiet reassurance, and a deeper understanding of the importance of belonging.

With hope,

Adorae

Once Upon A Time, at the edge of the woods, in a cosy cottage with beautiful flowers outside the front door, lived Mr and Mrs Honey Pot. They weren't just ordinary bears — they were **foster carers**. That means they looked after children who needed a safe and caring place to stay for a little while.

One day, two small children arrived with their bags. Ruby, who loved to twirl in her pink dress, and Bobby, who always wore his Bear United football shirt, looked a little nervous and unsure. But Mrs. Honey Pot was very kind. She welcomed them warmly and said gently, "This is a safe place. You can stay here while the grown-ups figure out what's best for you."

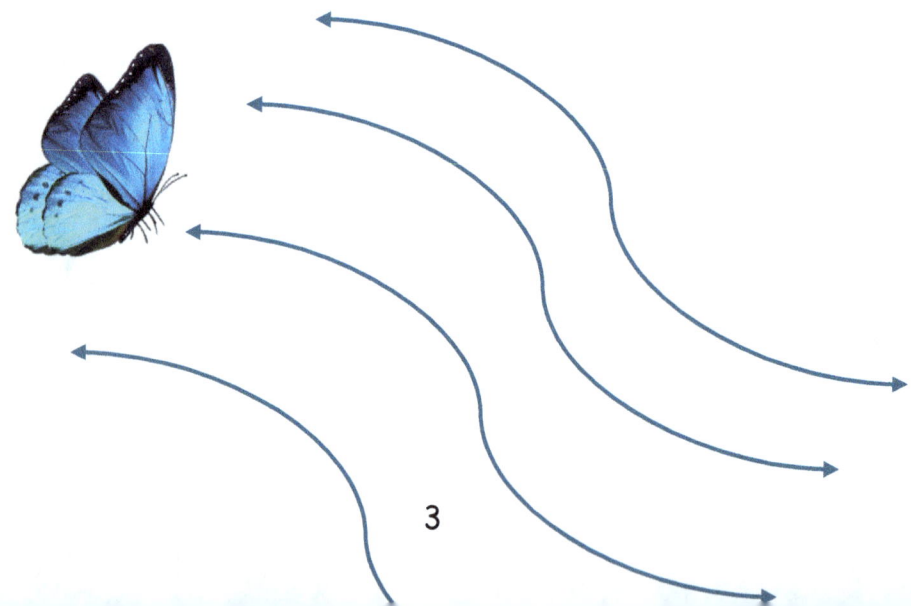

Ruby and Bobby couldn't live at home with their parents right now.

Sometimes, parents have a hard time keeping children safe — even when they love them very much. Some parents feel very sad inside, or get poorly in their minds or bodies. Some forget to cook food or wash clothes, or they sleep all day and don't wake up to help the children. Sometimes, parents have an illness or find learning things harder, and that can make it tricky for them to look after themselves or take care of a child properly.

Sometimes, parents use things like special drinks or strong medicine called **alcohol** or **drugs**. These can change the way a person feels and thinks. Some grown-ups use them when they feel very sad, or very worried, or when they don't know how to ask for help.

But when they use alcohol or drugs it can make it harder for them to look after children properly. So, they forget to cook food for the children, or take the children to school or to keep the children safe.

And sometimes, when parents are already feeling poorly or find it difficult to do things because of their illness or learning problems, alcohol and drugs can make it even harder for them to care for their children.

 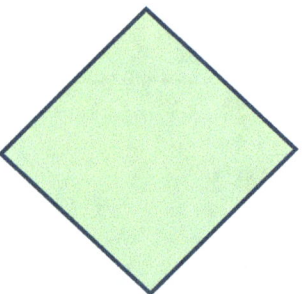

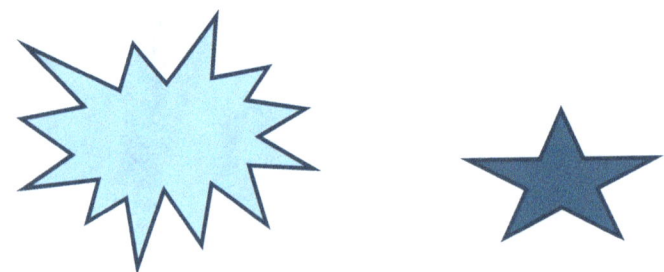

Sometimes, parents shout a lot or get very cross. They might slam doors, throw things, or say unkind words. Sometimes they hurt other people in the house — by pushing, hitting, or scaring them. This is called **domestic abuse** or **domestic violence**. When that happens, the children stop feeling safe at home. And that is never okay.

Children should never be around scary fighting or shouting. They should never have to hide in another room, or feel afraid, or try to fix the problem.

Even when parents are poorly or struggling, it's never a child's job to make things better. It's always the grown-ups' job to make sure that the children are safe, happy and well cared for.

It is never the children's fault. Not ever.

Sometimes, the safest thing is for children to stay with someone else in a different home - just for a little while - until their parents can get the help they need.

Ruby and Bobby hadn't done anything wrong. They just needed to stay in a safe house, a place full of love and care.

"We'll look after you while you're here," said Mr Honey Pot kindly. "There will be warm porridge in the mornings, cosy bedtime stories at night, and plenty of toys and games to enjoy."

Ruby twirled around in her sparkly dress, her pink bow bouncing as she laughed. Bobby banged his wooden spoon like a drum and hugged his football close.

With toys scattered around, and a big kitchen filled with yummy smells, Ruby and Bobby began to feel safe, cared for, and even a little bit happy.

Every child in foster care has a **social worker**. That's a special person whose job is to make sure children are safe, happy, and listened to. Ruby had one. Bobby did too.

The social workers visited them often to play games, draw pictures, and ask questions like, *"How are you feeling?"* and *"Do you have everything you need?* And *"If you had a magic wand what would you wish for? "*

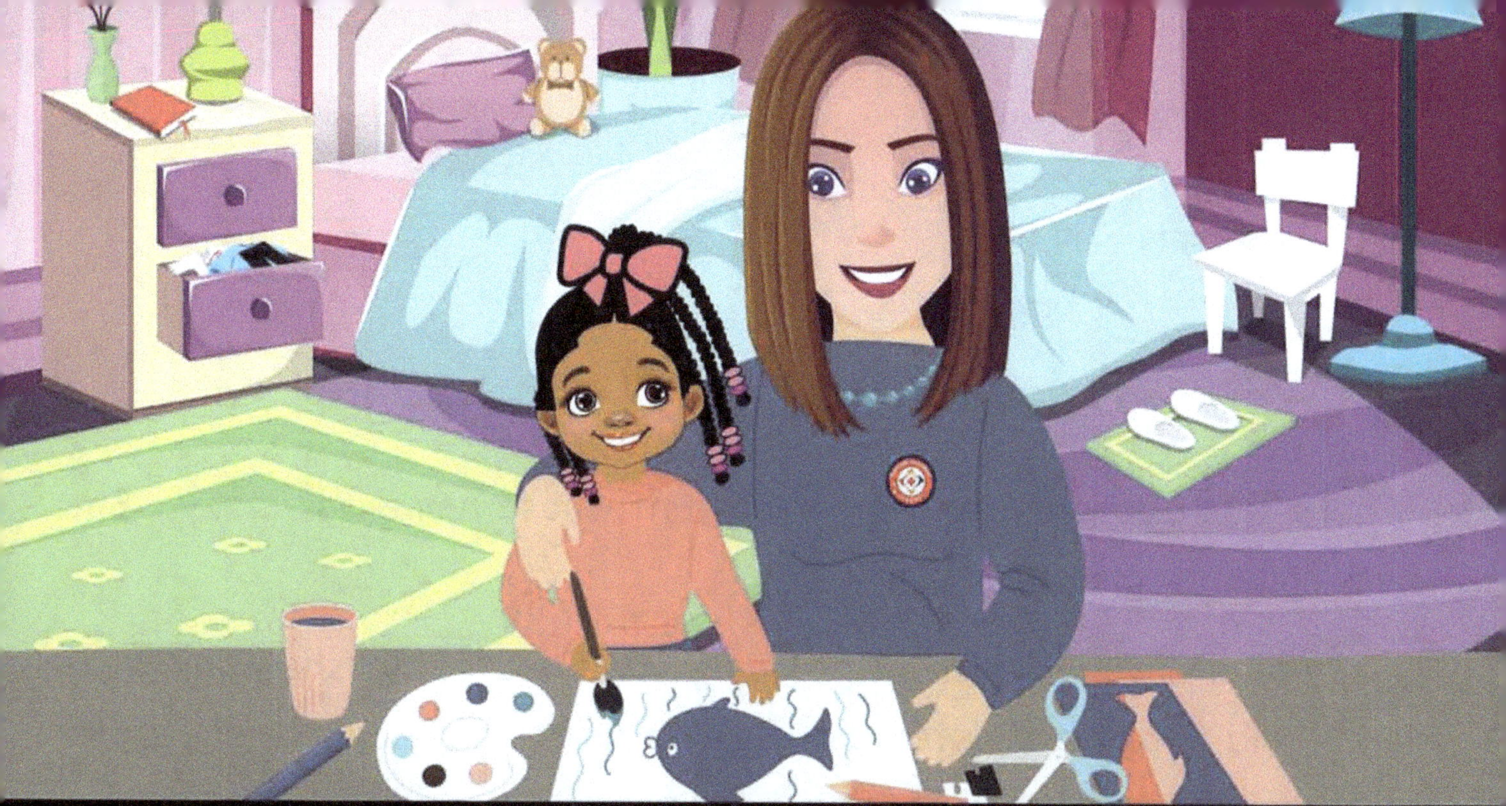

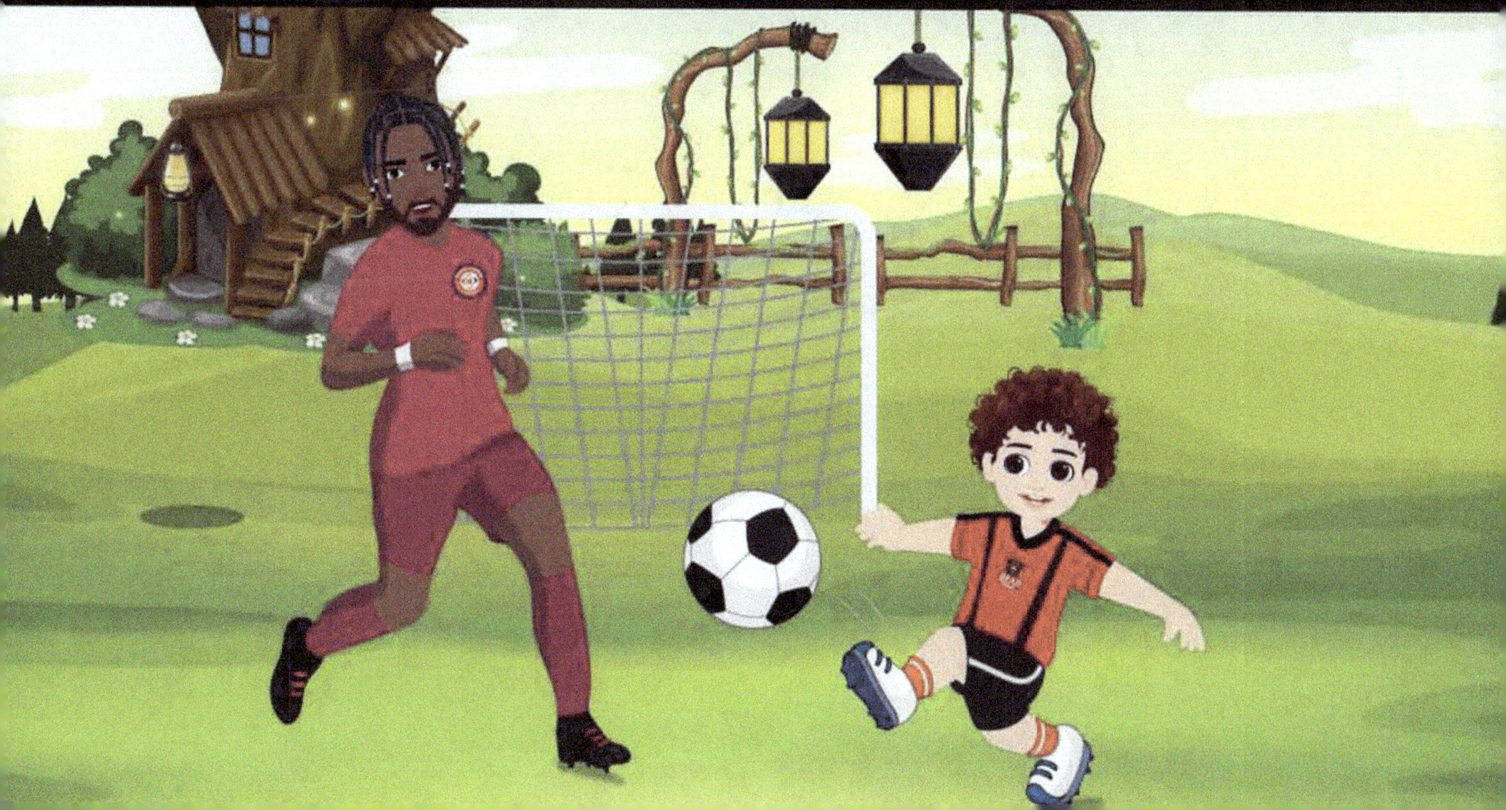

There was also someone very important whose name was Lizzy. She was called a **court guardian**.

Lizzy didn't live in Mr and Mrs Honey Pot's house, but she would visit Ruby and Bobby and listen carefully to what they said, so she could write a report about what is best for them.

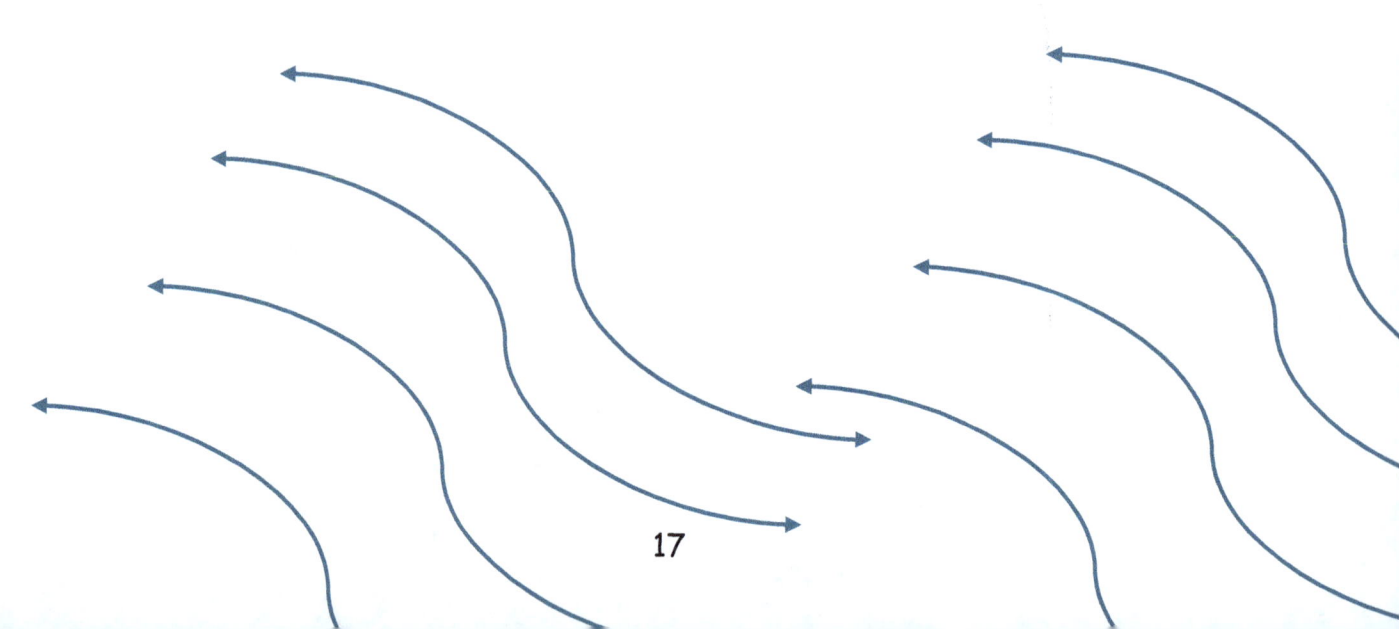

And then there was the **judge**. The judge wore special robes and worked in a quiet room called a **court**.

His job was to listen to everyone and read lots of reports from the social workers, the parents, the guardian, and also the children before making a very big decision about where the children should live so they will be safe, happy and well cared for.

The judge asked questions like:

"Can Ruby and Bobby go back home when it's safe?"

"Do they need to stay in foster care a bit longer?"

"Or should they find a new forever family?"

The judge always tries to choose what's best for the children.

Ruby and Bobby missed their mummy and daddy. When it was safe, they had **supervised contact** with their social worker nearby. Ruby loved showing her drawings, Bobby liked telling stories and sometimes there were even little cupcakes to share.

Life at the Honey Pot Home began to feel a little easier.

Ruby twirled through the garden like a dancer.

Bobby kicked footballs through hoops and made up his own goal songs.

At bedtime, Mrs Honey Pot tucked them in and whispered,

"You are safe. You are loved. You are not alone."

No one knew just yet what the judge would decide. But Ruby and Bobby knew one very important thing: There were kind grown-ups all around them, helping them take one brave step at a time.

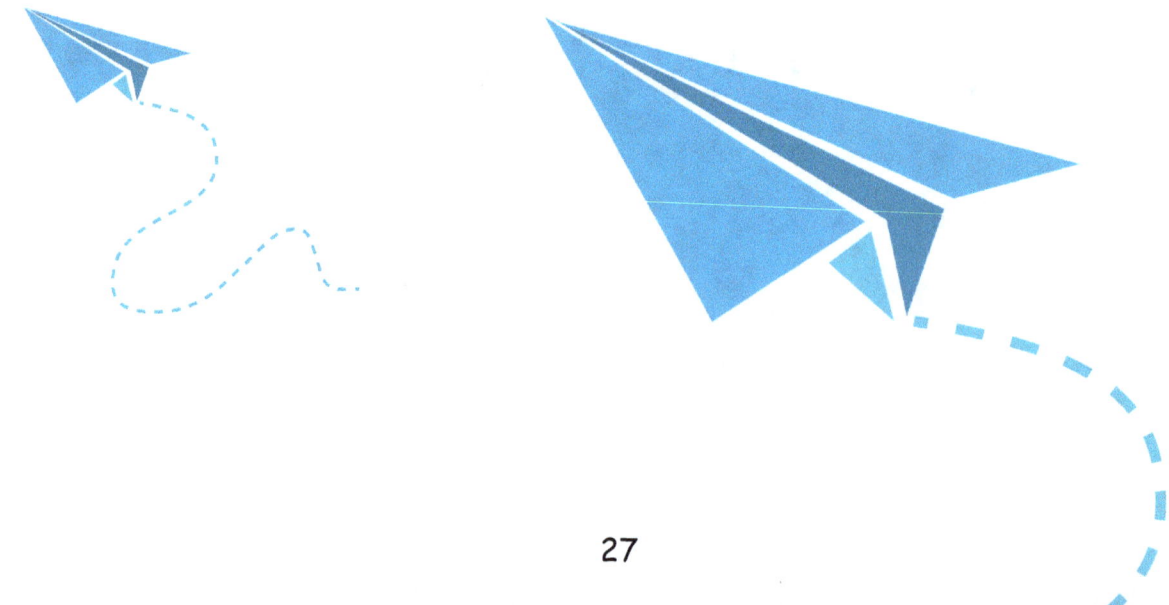

And wherever their path would lead, Mr and Mrs Honey Pot would always be cheering for them. Because all they needed was a little love... And a safe place to grow.

The End